HEADQUARTERS, U. S. MARINE CORPS
WASHINGTON, D. C. 20380-0001

Users Manual (UM) for the On-Line Diary System (OLDS)

Users Manual

18 April 1986
MPI Document Number
UM-OLDS
Version 1.00

Prepared by
Manpower Management Information Systems Branch
Manpower Department
Headquarters, U. S. Marine Corps
Washington, D. C. 20380-0001

E R R A T U M

ON-LINE DIARY SYSTEM

USERS MANUAL

Please add distribution code EC5 to the distribution page.

DISTRIBUTION: DX3, EC5

Copy to:

CMC (Asst to DC/S for Mpr), Washington, DC 20380-0001	1
CMC (M-1), Washington, DC 20380-0001	1
CMC (MH), Washington, DC 20380-0001	1
CMC (MR), Washington, DC 20380-0001	1
CMC (MMPR), Washington, DC 20380-0001	1
CMC (MMOS), Washington, DC 20380-0001	1
CMC (MMRB), Washington, DC 20380-0001	1
CMC (MMPE), Washington, DC 20380-0001	1
CMC (MMPR), Washington, DC 20380-0001	1
CMC (MMOS), Washington, DC 20380-0001	1
CMC (MMOA), Washington, DC 20380-0001	1
CMC (MMEA), Washington, DC 20380-0001	1
CMC (MPI-10), Washington, DC 20380-0001	1
CMC (MPI-20), Washington, DC 20380-0001	1
CMC (MPI-30), Washington, DC 20380-0001	1
CMC (MPI-40), Washington, DC 20380-0001	5
CMC (MPI-50), Washington, DC 20380-0001	1
CMC (MPI-60), Washington, DC 20380-0001	1
CMC (RESM), Washington, DC 20380-0001	1
CMC (CCI), Washington, DC 20380-0001	1
Dir, MCCDPA (Code 09A), Quantico, VA 22143-5001	1
Dir, MCCDPA (Code 09B), Quantico, VA 22143-5001	1
Dir, MCCDPA (Code 09F), Quantico, VA 22143-5001	1
Dir, MCCDPA (Code TPPS), Kansas City, MO 64197-0501	1
Each ACU	5
CO, MCFC (MPI-LNU), Kansas City, MO 64197-0001	1
CO, MCFC (RFAM), Kansas City, MO 64197-0001	1
CO, MCFC (M), Kansas City, MO 64197-0001	1
CO, NPRDC (Code 61), San Diego, CA 92152-6800	1
CO, NPRDC (Code 622), San Diego, CA 92152-6800	1
Supt, NPS (Code 54Dk), Monterey, CA 93943-5100	1
Supt, NPS (Code 0306), Monterey, CA 93943-5100	1
DSA, 350 Fortune Terrace, Rockville, MD 20854-2995	1
Ideamatics, 1806 T St., N.W., Washington, DC 20009	1
PAC, Suite 350, 1300 N. 17th St., Arlington, VA 22209	1
MTT, Camp Lejeune, NC 28542-0001	1
CO, PA School, Camp Lejeune, NC 28542-0001	1

PCN 100 000 015 30

RECORD OF CHANGES

Change Number	Date of Change	Date Received	Date Entered	Signature of Person Entering Change

LIST OF EFFECTIVE PAGES

Page Number	Version
Cover	1.00
Record of Changes Page	1.00
List of Effective Pages Page	1.00
i to v	1.00
1 to 50	1.00
A-1 to A-3	1.00
Distribution Page	1.00

TABLE OF CONTENTS

SECTION/PARAGRAPH PAGE

TABLE OF CONTENTS

TABLE OF CONTENTS

SECTION/PARAGRAPH PAGE

Chapter 3. PREPARER'S INSTRUCTIONS

FIGURE

TABLE OF CONTENTS

TABLE OF CONTENTS

SECTION/PARAGRAPH PAGE

Chapter 1

INTRODUCTION AND SIGN-ON PROCEDURES

1001. Purpose and Function of the On-line Diary System

1. The purpose of the On-line Diary System (OLDS) is to serve as the mechanism for collection of data for input to the REAL FAMMIS data base and includes all feedback pertaining to that input. Specifically, the OLDS will:

a. Provide the user the capability to input information through transaction production to update the REAL FAMMIS data base.

b. Provide for thorough and accurate detection of errors in a timely manner which will enable errors to be corrected within minimal timeframes.

c. Provide the user the capability to review and certify reported data.

d. Provide a controlled means of inputting data for processing, updating the master records, and updating historical/advisory feedback data to the originator.

e. Assist the user with as much "generated/prompted" information as required to enable accurate and timely input, research, correction, and audit of functional data.

2. The function of the OLDS supports both administrative and disbursing personnel in accomplishment of their respective duties. The major functions performed by the OLDS includes the preparation of diaries and payrolls; the ability to detect and correct errors; certification of the completed diaries; input of the certified data into the update cycle; retention of the transaction/payment data for audit purposes; and the ability to provide feedback statistics pertaining to the system's performance.

1002. Commanding Officer's (CO) Responsibilities. CO responsibilities are outlined in chapter two.

1003. Preparer's Responsibilities. Preparer's responsibilities are outlined in chapter three.

1004. Certifier's Responsibilities. Certifier's responsibilities are outlined in chapter four.

1005. Sign-On and Log-On at the Local Regional Automated Services Center (RASC)

1. Diary System: This system is located at the local RASC. To access the system, complete the following steps: The message "MARINE CORPS DATA NETWORK IS ACTIVE, ENTER MENU TO ACCESS ACF/VTAM APPLICATIONS PROGRAM" will appear on the screen (see figure 1-1). 1) Type in "MENU" (without the quotations) and press "ENTER." The local applications screen will appear. In figure 1-2 this is the Quantico application. 2) To access Quantico, select Option 01 (COM-PLETE) and press "ENTER." The message "THIS TERMINAL IS CONNECTED TO COMPLETE" will appear on the screen (see figure 1-3). 3) Type *ULOG ON, the six-character user-ID, and press "ENTER." The message "ENTER YOUR TOP SECRET PASSWORD/NEWPASSWORD" will appear on the screen (see figure 1-4). 4) Enter your password and press "ENTER". (NOTE: User passwords are not visible on the display screen when being entered). The TOP SECRET user-ID screen will appear (see figure 1-5), press "ENTER" to continue. The COMPLETE --- BROADCAST screen for the local RASC will appear (see figure 1-6). This screen is controlled by the local RASC and may contain messages relative to the status of the system and should be read carefully. 5) Press "ENTER", and the COMPLETE COM-PASS screen will appear (see figure 1-7). 6) You may select one of the following options: OLDV (A); MESSAGE SWITCHING (B); or USER INFO (C). Option (A) will allow the user to start, continue, or review diaries. Option (C) allows the user to send and receive messages under their own unit mailbox. Option (B) allows the user to send and receive messages from other diary users on an individual basis. 7) After selecting Option (A) (OLDV), press "ENTER", and a message screen will appear (see figure 1-8). This screen is controlled by the local Administrative Control Unit (ACU) and may contain messages that are pertinent to all units. 8) Press "ENTER" to continue. The ON-LINE DIARY MASTER MENU will appear (see figure 1-9).

1006. Sign-On and Log-On at Marine Corps Central Design and Programming Activity (MCCDPA)

1. Printing Reports System. This system is located at MCCDPA, Kansas City, MO. To access this system complete the following steps: The message "MARINE CORPS DATA NETWORK IS ACTIVE, ENTER MENU TO ACCESS ACF/VTAM APPLICATIONS PROGRAM" will appear on the screen (see figure 1-1). 1) Enter "MENU" (without the quotations) and press "ENTER." The MENU screen will appear (see figure 1-2). 2) To access KCTCOMPLETE (KCMO) select item 27 and press "ENTER." The KCT APPLICATIONS screen will appear. Select item 02 and press "ENTER" (see figure 1-14). The message "THIS TERMINAL IS CONNECTED TO MCCDPA, KC, MO. COMPLETE" will appear on the screen (see figure 1-10). 3) Enter *ULOG ON, the six-character user-ID code, and press "ENTER." The message "ENTER YOUR TOP SECRET PASSWORD/NEW PASSWORD" will appear on the screen

(see figure 1-4). 4) Enter your password and press "ENTER" (NOTE: User passwords are not visible on the display screen when being entered). If either an incorrect user-ID code or password has been entered, the appropriate message "USER-ID RECORD NOT ON FILE" or "PASSWORD IS INCORRECT, PLEASE PRESS "ENTER" TO CONTINUE" will appear on the screen. In either event, repeat the log-on procedure. The TOP SECRET user-ID screen will appear (see figure 1-5), press "ENTER" to continue. When the log-on is successful, the screen will display a KCMOPROD --- BROADCAST screen (see figure 1-11). This screen is controlled by MCCDPA, Kansas City, MO, and may contain messages relative to the status of the system and should be read carefully. 5) Press "ENTER" and the KCMOPROD COM-PASS screen will appear (see figure 1-12). You may select one of the following options: VIS (A); ASSIST (B); or OLDV (C). Option A (VIS) (Video Inquiry System) allows the user to screen a Marine's JUMPS/MMS/REMMPS record for research purposes. Option B (User Assistance) allows the user to review messages that disbursing and ACU send. Option A will be further explained in chapter 6, (section 2). Option C (OLDV) is used to retrieve the on-line reports. 6) Enter "C" (without the quotations) and press "ENTER." The On-line Diary Master Menu will be displayed on the screen (see figure 1-13). 7) Select one of the following options:

a. Option A (Diary System) will take the user to the On-line Sign On (ELSIG, SEED and RUC) screen. Chapter 2 explains subsequent steps for the commanding officer. Chapter 3 explains subsequent steps for the diary preparer. Chapter 4 explains subsequent steps for the certifying officer.

b. Option B (Diary Statistics Report) provides the user with the current status of the unit/disbursing diaries. The RUC/DSSN must be entered with Option B. Available at MCCDPA, Kansas City, MO, ONLY.

c. Option C (Error Report) provides the user with the Error Report for his unit/disbursing diaries. The RUC/DSSN must be entered with Option C. If all errors are desired, move the cursor to CYCNR and press the "ERASE EOF" key to remove the zeroes, then press "ENTER." If errors for a particular cycle are needed, move the cursor to CYCNR and enter the particular cycle desired, then press "ENTER." The user must key in a "Y" in the PRTOPT field in order for the requested report to print out on a printer.

d. Option D (Advisory Report) provides the user with the Advisory Report for his unit/disbursing office. The RUC/DSSN must be entered with Option D. If all advisories are desired, move the cursor to CYCNR and press the "ERASE EOF" key to remove the zeroes, then press "ENTER." If advisories for a particular cycle are needed, move the cursor to CYCNR and enter the cycle number desired, then press "ENTER." The user must key in a "Y" in the PRTOPT field in order for the requested report to print out on a printer.

e. Option E (Unit/Disbursing Reports) will take the user to the Unit/Disbursing Reports Menu Screen. Available at MCCDPA, Kansas City, MO, ONLY.

f. Option F (MPV/MPL Statistics Report) will take the user to the MPV/MPL Statistics Report Menu Screen. Available at MCCDPA, Kansas City, MO, ONLY.

g. Option G provides the user with a listing of current TTC codes in TTC sequence.

h. Option H provides the user with a listing of current TTC codes in English.

1007. Network Control Centers (NCC)

1. The OLDS uses the Marine Corps Data Network (MCDN) to connect users with the central computer in Kansas City. Network Control Centers have been established at each Regional Automated Services Center (RASC) to support MCDN users and to assist users with hardware and telephone problems. These centers are manned at all times to support the user. Users should contact the closest Network Control Center when they encounter hardware and telephone line problems in using the OLDS.

2. Network Control Centers:

	COMMERCIAL	AUTOVON
MCCDPA Kansas City	816 926-5265/7439	465-5265/7439
MCCDPA Quantico	703 640-2648/2588	278-2648/2588
HQMC Washington	202 694-3039/4878	224-3039/4878
MCCDPA Albany	912 439-5173/6648	460-5173/6648
RASC Camp Pendleton	619 725-4676/3721	993-3787/3721
RASC Camp Lejeune	919 451-1019/2308	484-1019/2308
MCRSC Overland Park	913 236-3185	465-3185

If the NCC is unable to assist, the user will be referred to the appropriate Administrative Control Unit (ACU) or in case of the disbursing system, the Electronic Signature Security Officer, MCFC, Kansas City, MO, (AUTOVON 465-7281, COMMERCIAL (816) 926-7281) or the Deputy Electronic Signature Security Officer, MCFC, Kansas City, MO, (AUTOVON 465-5424, COMMERCIAL (816) 926-5424).

1008. Log-Off

1. Enter Option 99 from any Master Function Menu screen, or from the commander's authority module when exiting the diary system under the local RASC. The On-line Diary Master Menu will be displayed on the screen. Press the "CLEAR" key, the COMPLETE COM-PASS screen will appear. Key in *ULOG OFF and press "ENTER." A "LOG-OFF SUCCESSFUL" message will be displayed on the screen. The system will automatically display the screen shown in figure 1-2. The terminal is now successfully logged-off.

2. Press the "CLEAR" key from any Master Menu screen when exiting the MCCDPA Diary Reports System. The KCMOPROD COM-PASS screen will appear. Enter *ULOG OFF and press "ENTER." A "LOG-OFF SUCCESSFUL" message will be displayed. The system will automatically display the screen shown in figure 1-2. The terminal is now successfully logged-off.

```
(HQI) MARINE CORPS DATA NETWORK IS ACTIVE           TERMINAL ID=@
  ENTER  MENU   TO ACCESS ACF/VTAM APPLICATION PROGRAMS
```

Figure 1-1.--Example of Marine Corps Data Network Screen.

```
TERM:     GIC2BA02    DATE: 01/06/86    COMM: 690-1234
LOGMODE: LUO          TIME:  8:42:45    AUT:  278-2156
*********************** QUANTICO APPLICATIONS *****************
01 COM-PLETE               0600/0300 COMP 13
02 ROSCOE                  0600/0300 ROSC 14
03 TSO                     0600/0300 TSO  15
04 CSS ROSCOE              0600/0300 CSS  16
05 PHOENIX                 0600/0300 PHOE 17
06 COM-PLETE5              0600/0300 COM5 18
07 CICS                    0600/0300 CICS 19
08 KCTCOMPLETE             0600/0300 KCTC 20
09 KCMO COMTRAIN           0600/0300 KCCO 21
10 KCMO ROSCOE1            0600/0300 KCR1 22
11 KCMO ROSCOE2            0600/0300 KCR2 23
12                                        24
************************** NETWORK NODES **********************
25 KCTMENU      KCT      29 ALAMENU      ALA      33  OKRMENU  OKR
26 RFCMENU      RFC      30 CLBMENU      CLB      34
27 MQGMENU      MQG      31 HIFMENU      HIF      35
28 MQGMENU      HQI      32 CPPMENU      CPP      36
***************************************************************
PLEASE ENTER SELECTION BELOW (PRESS PF KEY 1 FOR HELP)

SELECTION=
```

Figure 1-2.--Example of a Local Applications Screen.

```
ZVT0003 - THIS TERMINAL IS CONNECTED TO COM-PLETE.
```

Figure 1-3.--Sample COM-PLETE Connection Screen.

```
TSS753A ENTER YOUR TOP SECRET PASSWORD/NEWPASSWORD
```

Figure 1-4.--Sample TOP SECRET Password Screen.

```
TSS701I GMPI49  LAST-USED 03 JAN 86 04:56 SYSTEM=TTOB FACILITY=
  COMPLETE  TSS702I COUNT=00335 MODE=WARN  LOCKTIME=030 NAME=
  BRADFORD, J. R. MSGT

  *** PLEASE HIT ENTER KEY TO CONTINUE ***
```

Figure 1-5.--Sample TOP SECRET User-ID Screen.

```
ULG0016 - LOGON SUCCESSFUL

GMPI49 TID=2872 ACCT=MPI-40 AUTH=9000 RMC=1,2 SMC=1 NONCONTROL
       TIMEON=08:42:10
*********************  COMPLETE  ---  BROADCAST  ***************
*                                                              *
*         MARINE CORPS DESIGN AND PROGRAMMING ACTIVITY         *
*                      QUANTICO, VIRGINIA                      *
*                                                              *
*     HOURS OF INTERACTIVE SERVICE (QUANTICO LOCAL TIMES)      *
*        0001-0300, 0700-2400 MONDAY THROUGH THURSDAY          *
*               0001-0300, 0700-2000 FRIDAY                    *
*           0700-1500 SATURDAY      1800-2400 SUNDAY           *
*        FOR PROBLEMS CALL YOUR LOCAL USER HELP DESK           *
*                                                              *
*   %%  WARNING  %%  WARNING  %%  WARNING  %%  WARNING  %%     *
*                                                              *
*   SPOOLED PRINT OUT MAY BE LOST AFTER 48 HOURS IF IT IS NOT  *
*   PRINTED OFF.  THERE IS A DOCUMENT ADDRESSING LIMIT FOR     *
*   SPOOLED DATA TO THE DISK AREA COM-PLETE USES.  WITH        *
*   INCREASE IN USERS, WRAP-AROUND OCCURS AT A MINIMUM EVERY   *
*   36 HOURS AT PRESENT.  IT IS THE USER'S RESPONSIBILITY TO   *
*   ENSURE THAT THEIR PRINTERS ARE OPERATIONAL, IE, TURNED ON, *
*   TO ALLOW ANY SPOOLED PRINT TO BE PRINTED OUT.  IF 2 DAY    *
*   OLD PRINT DISAPPEARS, THIS IS THE REASON.                  *
****************************************************************
```

Figure 1-6.--Sample COMPLETE Broadcast Screen.

```
06:46:49     TID  2872     COMPLETE     USER ID GMPI49       01/06/86
                        -- COM-PASS --                           USTK

    SUSPENDED PROGRAMS            PROGRAM SERVICES
--------------------------   ------------------------------------
PROGRAM   NAME   LEVEL  PF   SERVICE DESCRIPTION  PROGRAMS  ID PF
-------   ----   -----  --   -------------------  --------  -- --
                             ONLINE DIARY DRIVER  OLDV       A 04
                             MESSAGE SWITCHING    UM         B
                             USER INFO            UINFO      C
```

Figure 1-7.--Sample COMPLETE COM-PASS Screen.

```
***********************************************************
* A T T E N T I O N  A L L  U N I T  D I A R Y  U S E R S *
***********************************************************
851218: XXXXXXXXXXXXXXXXXXXXXXXXXXXXXXXXXXXXXXXXXXXXXXXXXXX
XXXXXXXXXXXXXXXXXXXXXXXXXXXXXXXXXXXXXXXXXXXXXXXXXXXXXXXXXXX
XXXXXXXXXXXXXXXXXXXXXXXXXXXXXXXXXXXXXXXXXXXXXXXXXXXXXXXXXXX

851221: XXXXXXXXXXXXXXXXXXXXXXXXXXXXXXXXXXXXXXXXXXXXXXXXXXX
XXXXXXXXXXXXXXXXXXXXXXXXXXXXXXXXXXXXXXXXXXXXXXXXXXXXXXXXXXX
XXXXXXXXXXXXXXXXXXXXXXXXXXXXXXXXXXXXXXXXXXXXXXXXXXXXXXXXXXX
XXXXXXXXXXXXXXXXXXXXXXXXXXXXXXXXXXXXXXXXXXXXXXXXXXXXXXXXXXX
XXXXXXXXXXXXXXXXXXXXXXXXXXXXXXXXXXXXXXXXXXXXXXXXXXXXXXXXXXX
XXXXXXXXXXXXXXXXXXXXXXXXXXXXXXXXXXXXXXXXXXXXXXXXXXXXXXXXXXX

851226: XXXXXXXXXXXXXXXXXXXXXXXXXXXXXXXXXXXXXXXXXXXXXXXXXXX
XXXXXXXXXXXXXXXXXXXXXXXXXXXXXXXXXXXXXXXXXXXXXXXXXXXXXXXXXXX
XXXXXXXXXXXXXXXXXXXXXXXXXXXXXXXXXXXXXXXXXXXXXXXXXXXXXXXXXXX
XXXXXXXXXXXXXXXXXXXXXXXXXXXXXXXXXXXXXXXXXXXXXXXXXXXXXXXXXXX
XXXXXXXXXXXXXXXXXXXXXXXXXXXXXXXXXXXXXXXXXXXXXXXXXXXXXXXXXXX
XXXXXXXXXXXXXXXXXXXXXXXXXXXXXXXXXXXXXXXXXXXXXXXXXXXXXXXXXXX
XXXXXXXXXXXXXXXXXXXXXXXXXXXXXXXXXXXXXXXXXXXXXXXXXXXXXXXXXXX

851229: XXXXXXXXXXXXXXXXXXXXXXXXXXXXXXXXXXXXXXXXXXXXXXXXXXX
XXXXXXXXXXXXXXXXXXXXXXXXXXXXXXXXXXXXXXXXXXXXXXXXXXXXXXXXXXX
```

Figure 1-8.--Sample Local Application Message Screen.

```
01/06/86      QUANTICO VSAM ONLINE DIARY MASTER MENU      08:59:12
    OPTION    DESCRIPTION                 PARAMETERS
-----------------------------------------------------------------
      A       DIARY SYSTEM


                            OPTION:  A
                               RUC:
                              DSSN:

AFTER ENTERING YOUR INQUIRY DATA ABOVE, DEPRESS THE ENTER KEY.
IF YOU DO NOT WANT THIS SCREEN, ENTER THE APPROPRIATE PF KEY OR
DEPRESS CLEAR.
```

Figure 1-9.--Sample On-line Diary Master Menu.

```
ZVT0003 - THIS TERMINAL IS CONNECTED TO MCCDPA KC, MO. COMPLETE.
```

Figure 1-10.--Sample MCCDPA, MCFC, KCMO, COMPLETE Screen.

```
ULG0016 - LOGON SUCCESSFUL

GMPI49 TID=2872 ACCT=MPI-40 AUTH=9000 RMC=1,2 SMC=1 NONCONTROL
      TIMEON=08:42:10
*********************  KCMOPROD  ---  BROADCAST  ***************
* * * * * * * * * *    STOP AND READ THIS MESSAGE ! ! !  * * * *
* xxxxxxxxxxxxxxxxxxxxxxxxxxxxxxxxxxxxxxxxxxxxxxxxxxxxxxxxxxxxx *
* xxxxxxxxxxxxxxxxxxxxxxxxxxxxxxxxxxxxxxxxxxxxxxxxxxxxxxxxxxxxx *
* xxxxxxxxxxxxxxxxxxxxxxxxxxxxxxxxxxxxxxxxxxxxxxxxxxxxxxxxxxxxx *
* xxxxxxxxxxxxxxxxxxxxxxxxxxxxxxxxxxxxxxxxxxxxxxxxxxxxxxxxxxxxx *
* xxxxxxxxxxxxxxxxxxxxxxxxxxxxxxxxxxxxxxxxxxxxxxxxxxxxxxxxxxxxx *
* xxxxxxxxxxxxxxxxxxxxxxxxxxxxxxxxxxxxxxxxxxxxxxxxxxxxxxxxxxxxx *
*        *****  PRESS CLEAR TO CONTINUE   *****                 *
*****************************************************************
```

Figure 1-11.--Sample KCMOPROD Broadcast Screen.

```
06:46:49    TID  2872    KCMOPROD     USER ID GMPI49      01/06/86
                      -- COM-PASS --                          USTK

    SUSPENDED PROGRAMS           PROGRAM SERVICES
--------------------------   ------------------------------------
PROGRAM   NAME   LEVEL  PF   SERVICE DESCRIPTION  PROGRAMS   ID PF
-------   ----   -----  --   -------------------  --------   -- --
                   1    10   ONLINE DIARY VSAM    OLDV        A 01
                   2    11   USER ASSISTANCE      ASSIST      B 02
                   3    12   VIDEO INFO. SYSTEM   VIS         C 03

ENTER INPUT:
```

Figure 1-12.--Sample KCMOPROD COM-PASS Screen.

```
01/06/86        MCCDPA ONLINE DIARY MASTER MENU          07:50:46
                          VSAM DIARY

    OPTION     DESCRIPTION                  PARAMETERS
-----------------------------------------------------------------
      A        DIARY SYSTEM
      B        DIARY STATISTICS REPORT      RUC/DSSN
      C        ERROR REPORT                 RUC/DSSN
      D        ADVISORY REPORT              RUC/DSSN, (SCYCNR)
      E        UNIT/DISBURSING REPORTS      (RUC/DSSN)
      F        MPV/MPL STATISTICS REPORT    DSSN
      G        TTC/SEQ REPORT (BY TTC/SEQ)
      H        TTC/SEQ REPORT (BY ENGLISH)

                           OPTION: A
                              RUC:
                             DSSN:
                       PAYROLL NR:
                            CYCNR: 000  LAST COMPLETED: 270 851226
                           PRTOPT:      (USED WITH OPTION C/D ONLY)
                         PRT DEST: GIP3DA13

AFTER ENTERING YOUR INQUIRY DATA ABOVE, DEPRESS THE ENTER KEY.
IF YOU DO NOT WANT THIS SCREEN, ENTER THE APPROPRIATE PF KEY OR
DEPRESS CLEAR.
```

Figure 1-13.--Sample MCCDPA On-line Diary Master Menu.

```
TERM:     GIC2BA02   DATE: 02/06/86    HELP: 816-926-7439
LOGMODE: LUO         TIME:  8:42:45    NET:  926-7439
*********************** KCT      APPLICATIONS ******************
01 ROSCOE                 0200/2400 ROSC 13
02 COMPLETE               0001/2400 COMP 14
03 ARMS-PRODUCTION        0001/2400 ARMS 15
04 COMTEST                0001/2400 COMT 16
05 COMTRAIN               0001/2400 COMR 17
06 CICS-PRODUCTION        0700/1530 CICS 18
07 CICS-DEVELOPMENT       0700/1530 CICD 19
08 UCC-SEVEN              0001/2400 UCC7 20
09 TOP SECRET ADMIN       0200/2400 TASO 21
10                                       22
11                                       23
12                                       24
************************** NETWORK NODES ***********************
25 MQGMENU       MQG      29 ALAMENU      ALA      33  OKRMENU   OKR
26 HQIMENU       HQI      30 CLBMENU      CLB      34
27 KCTMENU       KCT      31 HIFMENU      HIF      35
28 RFCMENU       RFC      32 CPPMENU      CPP      36
****************************************************************
PLEASE ENTER SELECTION BELOW (PRESS PF KEY 1 FOR HELP)

SELECTION=
```

Figure 1-14.--Sample KCT Applications Menu Screen.

Chapter 2

MASTER AND CO ELECTRONIC SIGNATURE (ELSIG)

SECTION 1: MASTER ELSIG

2101. Master ELSIG. The Master ELSIG (M-ELSIG) is the code which identifies a particular unit and from which the CO ELSIG is generated. (Detailed instructions for the assignment of the CO ELSIG are contained in Section 2 of this chapter.) M-ELSIGS will be assigned by the REAL FAMMIS ELSIG Control Officer at HQMC (MPI-50).

1. The M-ELSIG is to be maintained and used only by the CO and must be carefully safeguarded at all times. It will be placed in a sealed envelope with the CO's signature over the flap and secured in a safe to which there is limited access. The envelope must be locked in a separate container if it is to be placed in a safe to which persons other than the CO have access. The CO will personally view the envelope containing the M-ELSIG at least once a week. Upon change of CO's, the M-ELSIG will be changed.

2. Should the M-ELSIG be compromised, suspected of compromise, or upon change of CO's, the REAL FAMMIS ELSIG Control Officer will be immediately notified. The REAL FAMMIS ELSIG Control Officer can be reached at the following telephone numbers (Comm: (202) 694-1971/4804; AUTOVON 224-1971/4804).

Chapter 2

SECTION 2: ASSIGNMENT OF COMMANDING OFFICER (CO) ELSIG

2201. CO ELSIG. The CO ELSIG is generated from the M-ELSIG and is utilized by the commanding officer to access the OLDS.

1. Upon assumption of duties, the CO must create his CO ELSIG. (See paragraph 2202, below.) This ELSIG should be considered as a personal signature and safeguarded as such. Should the CO ELSIG be suspected of compromise, the CO must change the ELSIG SEED and obtain a new CO ELSIG. (See paragraph 2202, below.)

2202. Detailed Instructions for Obtaining the CO ELSIG

1. Log-on the system at the local RASC, using the procedures set forth in chapter 1, paragraph 1005.

2. Key in the MASTER ELSIG and SEED. Press "ENTER."

3. Key in a Ø followed by your SSN. Key in a SEED. Select the proper identification code listed on the screen and key it in. Press "ENTER."

4. If your name does not appear automatically, key in LAST NAME, FIRST NAME and MIDDLE INITIAL. Utilize the "TAB FIELD FORWARD" key to position the cursor at the beginning of each field (see TAB FIELD FORWARD KEY in Glossary). Press "ENTER."

5. The CO ELSIG and SEED will be displayed for memorization.

6. Press "ENTER." The On-line System Sign-On Screen will be displayed. If you desire to assign P-ELSIGS enter your CO ELSIG and SEED, press "ENTER", and follow the instructions contained in Section 3 of this chapter (Electronic Signature Maintenance). If you desire to exit the system, leave the ELSIG and SEED blank and press "ENTER."

7. The On-line Diary Master Menu will be displayed. Log-off the system using the procedures set forth in chapter 1, subparagraph 1008.1.

Chapter 2

SECTION 3: CO FUNCTIONS

2301. <u>CO Functions</u>. The OLDS permits the CO to assign P-ELSIGS, review, certify, decertify and print diaries. The following procedures pertain to the CO functions.

1. Log-on the system using the procedures set forth in chapter 1, paragraph 1005. Select Option A and press "ENTER." The ELSIG, SEED, and RUC screen will appear.

2. Key in CO ELSIG, SEED, and RUC. Press "ENTER."

2302. <u>Options Available</u>. The following options are available to the CO:

10 - REVIEW, CERTIFY, OR DECERTIFY DIARY TRANSACTIONS
20 - ELECTRONIC SIGNATURE MAINTENANCE
99 - TERMINATE ON-LINE SYSTEM

1. <u>10 - REVIEW, CERTIFY, DECERTIFY</u>. Upon selection of this option the following screen will be displayed:

```
              REAL FAMMIS ON-LINE DIARY SYSTEM - MASTER MENU

*1.   START A NEW DIARY         (PREPARER ONLY)           (DEFAULT=N/A)
*2.   CONTINUE A DIARY          (PREPARER ONLY)           (DEFAULT=N/A)
*3.   REVIEW A DIARY            (PREPARER ONLY)           (DEFAULT=N/A)
                THERE ARE NO DIARIES AVAILABLE FOR REVIEW.
---------------------------------------------------------------------
 4.   REVIEW AND CERTIFY A DIARY  (CERTIFIER ONLY) (DEFAULT=00003)
 5.   DECERTIFY A DIARY           (CERTIFIER ONLY) (DEFAULT-N/A)
---------------------------------------------------------------------
 6.   PRINT A DIARY              (PRESS PF2 TO SEE AVAILABLE DIARIES)
---------------------------------------------------------------------
SELECT DESIRED OPTION=== 4
   INPUT DIARY NUMBER===                (LEAVE BLANK TO ACCEPT DEFAULT
                                        NUMBER

   INPUT DIARY DATE=== 860214           (USED FOR OPTION 1 ONLY)
     PRINTER=== 0223                    (ENTER TID TO ALTER PRINT
                                        DESTINATION)
----PF1 - MASTER FUNCTION MENU          PF2 = DIARY STATISTICS REPORT

USAMENUA - ENTER THE APPROPRIATE DATA ABOVE FOR THE OPTION
DESIRED. ONCE YOU HAVE ENTERED THE DATA NEEDED, DEPRESS THE ENTER
KEY TO CONTINUE.
```

*Not Applicable to Certifier.

a. <u>4 - REVIEW AND CERTIFY A DIARY</u>. Accept the system default and press "ENTER" if you desire to review/certify the system default diary. If you desire to review/certify another diary listed, position the cursor to the input diary number field and key in the diary number. Press "ENTER." The following ELSIG/SEED RE-ENTRY screen will appear prior to actual certification/deletion of a diary:

```
        REAL FAMMIS ON-LINE DIARY SYSTEM - ELSIG/SEED RE-ENTRY
                        CERTIFICATION/DELETION
DSSN:                        DIARY NUMBER:     DIARY DATE:  860214

1.   THIS DIARY WAS LAST TOUCHED AT 09:30:06 ON 14FEB86.  IF YOU
     WANT TO REVIEW THIS DIARY PRIOR TO TAKING ANY ACTION, PLEASE
     ENTER (YES) WITHOUT ENTERING YOUR ELSIG AND SEED.

2.   IF YOU WANT TO CERTIFY/DELETE THIS DIARY, PLEASE RE-ENTER YOUR
     ELSIG AND SEED.

3.   ONCE YOU HAVE ENTERED YOUR ELSIG AND SEED, DEPRESS THE ENTER
     KEY.

4.   IF YOU DO NOT WANT TO PERFORM THIS FUNCTION AT THIS TIME, LEAVE
     YOUR ELSIG AND SEED BLANK THEN DEPRESS YOUR ENTER KEY.

     DO YOU WANT TO REVIEW?  NO

        ELSIG:

        SEED:
```

If the DATE-TIME-GROUP on the above screen matches the DATE-TIME-GROUP of the reviewed hard copy diary, the certifier may take the NO option without reviewing each page of the diary. If the certifier desires to review each page of a diary, follow the instructions of Option 1 on the screen.

(1) If Option 1 is selected, the diary will be displayed with the statements listed as they were entered. Use the "TAB FIELD FORWARD" key to advance to each statement.

(a) To delete a statement, key in a "D", press "ENTER", and an asterisk will appear indicating the statement will be deleted.

(b) If no statements are marked for deletion, press "ENTER" to advance to the next page of the diary. A system default will always cause the next page of the diary to be displayed. After the entire diary has been reviewed the

Certification Screen will be displayed. If you desire to exit the review process prior to reviewing each page of the diary, move the cursor to the field following CONTINUE and key in NO. Press "ENTER." You will be returned to the Master MENU.

(c) After the review process has been completed you can certify the diary by entering your ELSIG and SEED on the certification screen. If you do not desire to certify the diary, leave the screen blank and press "ENTER." You will be returned to the Master Function Menu.

(d) The final copy of the diary will be printed, and the signed original will be submitted to the servicing ACU in accordance with current directives after the Diary Statistics Report indicates that the diary has been CLOSED or PROCESSED. The diary clerk has the capability to produce several working copies of diaries prior to certification or prior to final processing. Extreme care must be given to ensure that the final signed copy is retained as the official copy and not a rough working copy. The final copy can be easily identified since a message is printed at the top of the diary indicating that it has been submitted for processing. The working copies of the diary contain either of the following messages printed at the top of the page - ROUGH COPY DATA NOT CERTIFIED or ROUGH COPY - DATA NOT PROCESSED. The final signed copy of the diary will be filed in a separate binder and retained for one year as outlined in current directives.

(e) A diary can be deleted in its entirety by deleting all of the transactions on the diary and then entering the certification process. If the diary is empty, that is if all the entries have been deleted, then the certification process will cause a deletion screen to appear. A certifier can enter his ELSIG and SEED on the screen and delete the entire diary. If you do not wish to delete the diary leave the ELSIG and SEED blank and press "ENTER." You will be returned to the Master Function Menu. An entire diary should be deleted only in the case where an in- correct diary number or date is selected to start a new diary. For example, if diary 983 were started and the desired diary number was actually 9, then diary 983 could be deleted in its entirety.

b. <u>5 - DECERTIFY A DIARY</u>. Key in 5 and press "ENTER" if you desire to decertify the system default diary. If you desire to decertify another diary listed, position the cursor to the input diary number field and key in the desired diary number, press "ENTER." The ELSIG/SEED RE-ENTRY decertification screen will be displayed. Key in your ELSIG and SEED and press "ENTER." If you do not desire to decertify the diary, leave the ELSIG and SEED blank and press "ENTER." You will be returned to the Master Function Menu.

c. 6 - PRINT A DIARY. Key in 6 in the option field and the desired diary number in the INPUT DIARY NUMBER field. (Upon selection of option PF2 all diaries available for print, and their status will be displayed. Diaries are available for print for fifteen (15) days after the cycle completion date reflected on the Diary Statistics Report. Extreme care must be taken to ensure that diaries are printed prior to the drop-off date. Failure to do so will result in the unit being unable to print diaries. Commanders should contact the ACU for assistance when they are unable to print diaries. To return to the Master Function Menu, press "ENTER").

2. 20 - ELECTRONIC SIGNATURE MAINTENANCE. Upon selection of this option the screen in figure 2-1 will be displayed:

a. 10 - ASSIGN P-ELSIG AUTHORITY. This option (see figure 2-2) allows the CO to authorize specific individuals to prepare or to certify for his unit. The following instructions pertain:

(1) Key in a Ø followed by the individual's SSN, their authority and title identification. Press "ENTER."

(2) Key in the certifier/preparer's LAST NAME, FIRST NAME and MIDDLE INITIAL (if not already indicated), and the CO SEED in the spaces provided. (Position the cursor by use of the "FIELD TAB FORWARDED" key.) Press "ENTER."

(3) The ELSIG and SEED will be displayed for memorization.

(4) If more ELSIGS need to be assigned, Key in Y and press "ENTER." Return to the steps given above. If no more ELSIGS need to be assigned, key in N and you will be returned to the Electronic Signature Maintenance Screen. Press "ENTER."

b. 20 - CHANGE OWN ELSIG SEED. If you believe your ELSIG has been compromised, this option should be selected.

(1) Key in current SEED and select a new SEED. Press "ENTER." A new ELSIG will be generated.

(2) Memorize the new ELSIG and SEED. Press "ENTER." The Master Function Menu will be displayed.

c. 30 - REVIEW-DELETE P-ELSIG AUTHORITY. In this option the CO can review all personnel assigned Personal ELSIGS (P-ELSIGS) and delete specific individuals. (If a certifier or preparer forgets their ELSIG/SEED, the CO can delete the individual and assign a new ELSIG/SEED using Option 10, above. The SSN, NAME and AUTHORITY of all individuals assigned an ELSIG will be displayed. To delete an individual use the following procedures:

(1) Type a "D" in the space next to the SSN utilizing the "TAB FIELD FORWARD" key to position the cursor. Press "ENTER." The screen will reappear without the deleted individual.

(2) Upon completion of the P-ELSIG deletion/review, press "ENTER." You will be returned to the Electronic Signature Maintenance Screen.

d. 98 - RETURN TO MASTER ELSIG OPTIONS MENU. This option will return you to the CO Master Menu.

e. 99 - TERMINATE ON-LINE SYSTEM. Upon selection of this option, the On-line Diary Master Menu screen will be displayed.

(1) Press the "CLEAR" key. From the COM-PASS screen, key in *ULOG OFF and press "ENTER."

(2) A "LOG-OFF SUCCESSFUL" message will be displayed,

(3) Press the "ERASE EOF" key or "CLEAR" key. A terminal should not be left until this process has been successfully executed.

3. 99-TERMINATE ON-LINE SYSTEM. Key in 99 and press "ENTER." The On-line Diary Master Menu will be displayed. Log-off the system using the procedures set forth in chapter 1, subparagraph 1008.1.

```
     REAL FAMMIS ELECTRONIC SIGNATURE SYSTEM          EL2100V1
                    MAINTENANCE MODULE

SELECT OPTION====  10
10 : ASSIGN P-ELSIG AUTHORITY
20 : CHANGE OWN ELSIG SEED
30 : REVIEW/DELETE P-ELSIG AUTHORITY
98 : RETURN TO MASTER ELSIG OPTIONS MENU
99 : TERMINATE ONLINE SYSTEM
```

Figure 2-1.--Sample REAL FAMMIS Electronic Signature System Maintenance Module Screen.

```
    REAL FAMMIS ELECTRONIC SIGNATURE MAINTENANCE     EL2110V1
                ASSIGN PERSONAL ELSIGS
                SSN :

AUTHORITY : P          TITLE IDENTIFICATION CODE : E
                1 COMMANDING OFFICER
C : CERTIFIER   2 BY DIRECTION OF THE COMMANDING OFFICER
                3 BY DIRECTION OF THE BATTALION COMMANDING OFFICER
P : PREPARER    4 INSPECTOR INSTRUCTOR
                5 BY DIRECTION OF THE INSPECTOR INSTRUCTOR
E : RETURN TO   6 ACTING
    ELSIG       7 NCOIC
    MAINTENANCE 8 OFFICER IN CHARGE
    MENU        9 BY DIRECTION OF THE OFFICER IN CHARGE
                A DIRECTOR
                B BY DIRECTION OF THE DIRECTOR
                C BY DIRECTION OF THE REGIMENTAL COMMANDER
                D BY DIRECTION OF THE COMMANDING GENERAL
                E PREPARER

                  PRESS ENTER TO CONTINUE
```

Figure 2-2.--Sample REAL FAMMIS Electronic Signature Assign Personal ELSIGS Screen.

```
REAL FAMMIS ON-LINE ELECTRONIC SIGNATURE MAINTENANCE     EL1120V1
     MODULE TO CHANGE YOUR PERSONAL SEED
          ENTER YOUR CURRENT SEED:
          ENTER YOUR NEW SEED:
LEAVE CURRENT SEED BLANK TO TERMINATE TRANSACTION
                                           PRESS ENTER TO CONTINUE
```

Figure 2-3.--Sample REAL FAMMIS On-line Electronic Signature Maintenance Module to Change Your Personal SEED Screen.

Chapter 3

PREPARER'S INSTRUCTIONS

SECTION 1: OVERVIEW OF FUNCTIONS

3101. Introduction. A preparer is an individual assigned by the CO to prepare diaries for a specific unit. A preparer may open a diary and, prior to certification, make changes and additions to that diary. A preparer may review diaries, print diaries and change P-ELSIG. A preparer cannot obtain access to diaries that were opened by another preparer.

3102. Prepare-Review Diary Transactions

1. Prepare. Before approaching the on-line terminal, the diary preparer should have the diary supporting documents annotated with the applicable TTC and sequence numbers. There are two options available for diary preparation:

a. The first option is to start a new diary. If this option is selected the system will automatically default to the next diary number. If a diary, other than the system default diary is desired, that diary number must be keyed in prior to pressing "ENTER."

b. The second option is to continue an existing diary. A preparer can only continue a diary which he has opened and which has not been certified. If changes need to be made to a certified diary, it must first be decertified by a certifying officer.

2. Review. A preparer may only review diaries which he has opened and which have not been certified. A preparer may delete or add diary entries.

3103. Change Own Electronic Signature SEED. The SEED, combined with the individual's SSN, generates the preparer's ELSIG. If the preparer believes his ELSIG has been compromised, the SEED should be changed and a new ELSIG generated. For security reasons it is advisable to change your SEED and generate a new ELSIG every sixty (60) days.

Chapter 3

SECTION 2: DETAILED INSTRUCTIONS

3201. Preparer's Entry Process. To enter the preparer's function, use the following steps:

1. Log-on the system using the procedures set forth in chapter 1. The On-line Diary Master Menu screen will be displayed. Press "ENTER."

2. Key in your ELSIG, SEED, and RUC. Press "ENTER." The ELSIG and SEED will not be displayed due to security reasons.

3202. Detailed Instructions for the Diary Preparer. The following options are available:

10 - PREPARE-REVIEW DIARY TRANSACTIONS
20 - CHANGE OWN ELECTRONIC SIGNATURE
99 - TERMINATE ON-LINE SYSTEM

1. 10 - PREPARE-REVIEW DIARY TRANSACTIONS. Upon selection Of this option, the Master Function Menu will be displayed. The following options are available:

```
          REAL FAMMIS ON-LINE DIARY SYSTEM MASTER MENU:

 1...START A NEW DIARY          (PREPARER ONLY)-(DEFAULT = 00001)
 2...CONTINUE A DIARY           (PREPARER ONLY)-(DEFAULT = NONE)
 3...REVIEW A DIARY             (PREPARER ONLY)-(DEFAULT = NONE)
       THERE ARE NO DIARIES AVAILABLE FOR REVIEW.

*4...REVIEW AND CERTIFY A DIARY  (CERTIFIER ONLY)-(DEFAULT = N/A)
*5...DECERTIFY A DIARY           (CERTIFIER ONLY)-(DEFAULT = N/A)

 6...PRINT A DIARY            (PRESS PF2 TO SEE AVAILABLE DIARIES)

 SELECT DESIRED OPTION === 1
   INPUT DIARY NUMBER ===          (LEAVE BLANK TO ACCEPT DEFAULT
                                   NUMBER)
       INPUT DIARY DATE === 840214 (USED FOR OPTION 1 ONLY)
       PRINTER === 0223 (ENTER TID TO ALTER PRINT DESTINATION)
 ---PF1=MASTER FUNCTION MENU       PF2=DIARY STATISTICS REPORT

UDAMENUA-ENTER THE APPROPRIATE DATA ABOVE FOR THE OPTION DESIRED.
ONCE YOU HAVE ENTERED THE DATA NEEDED, DEPRESS THE "ENTER" KEY TO
CONTINUE.
```

*NOT APPLICABLE TO PREPARER

a. 1-START A NEW DIARY. Key in 1, press "ENTER." The system will automatically assign the new diary the system default diary number. The diary clerk must ensure that the system default diary number and system default diary date (the current date) are the correct diary number and date for the diary being prepared. If not, the diary clerk may enter another diary number or another diary date or both. If it is determined that the diary number or date was incorrect after pressing "ENTER", the diary clerk should refer to subparagraph 2302.1a(1)(e) of this Manual. The below options are available for diary preparation:

b. 2-CONTINUE A DIARY. Diaries available for continuation and review are the same. They are listed following Option 3 REVIEW A DIARY. If you desire to continue the system default diary, press "ENTER." If you desire to continue another diary listed, position the cursor, using the "Field Tab Forward" Key, to the diary number field and key in the desired diary number. The initial diary preparation screen will be displayed. Follow the procedures described in subparagraph 3202.1c, below.

c. 3-REVIEW A DIARY. Key in a 3 and press "ENTER" if you desire to review the system default diary number. If you desire to review another diary listed, key in the diary number and press "ENTER." The diary will be displayed with the statements listed as they were entered. Use the "TAB FIELD FORWARD" key to advance to each statement.

(1) To delete a statement key in a D, press "ENTER." An asterisk will appear indicating that the statement has been deleted.

(2) If no statements are marked for deletion or re-activation, a system default will cause the next page of the diary to be displayed upon pressing "ENTER." If you desire to exit the review process, move the cursor to the field following CONTINUE, and key in NO. Press "ENTER."

(3) When the review process is complete, press "ENTER", the Master Function Menu will be displayed.

d. 6-PRINT A DIARY. Key in 6 in the option field and the desired diary number in the INPUT DIARY NUMBER FIELD. (Upon selection of option PF2, all diaries available for print, and their status will be displayed. Diaries are available for print for fifteen (15) days after the cycle completion date reflected on the Diary Statistics Report. Extreme care must be taken to ensure that diaries are printed prior to the drop-off date. Failure to do so will result in the unit being unable to print diaries. Commanders should contact the ACU for assistance when they are unable to print diaries. To return to the Master Function Menu, press "ENTER.")

e. After selecting Option 1 or 2, press "ENTER" and the Diary Update screen will appear.

```
              REAL FAMMIS ON-LINE DIARY SYSTEM DIARY UPDATE


RUC:  DIARY NUMBER:  DIARY DATE:

-----------------------------------------------------------------

TYPE - TYPE OF INPUT          OPTION - STATEMENT OPTION

-----------------------------------------------------------------

 1......INDIVIDUAL             1......NORMAL
 2......GROUP                  2......CORRECTION
 3......EVENT                  3......DELETION AND ADD
 4......EXCLUSION              4......DELETE AS ERRONEOUS
 5......MASTER MENU            5......CORRECT DELETE AS ERRONEOUS
 6......MASTER FUNCTION MENU   6......GROUP/EXCLUSION
                                      MEMBER ENTRY
-----------------------------------------------------------------

  SELECT TYPE OF INPUT          === 1
  SELECT STATEMENT OF OPTION    === 1      (USED W/TYPES 1,2,3,4)

  INPUT TTC AND SEQUENCE        ===        (NOT NEEDED W/OPTION 6)
  SOCIAL SECURITY NUMBER        ===        (USED W/TYPE 1 ONLY)

  INPUT GROUP/EVENT NUMBER      ===        (USED W/TYPES 2,3,4)
  INPUT EXCLUSION NUMBER        ===        (USED W/TYPE 4 ONLY)

UDA0100A - ENTER THE APPROPRIATE DATA ABOVE FOR YOUR DESIRED
OPTIONS. AFTER ENTERING THE NECESSARY INFORMATION, DEPRESS THE
"ENTER" KEY TO CONTINUE.
```

(1) 1-INDIVIDUAL. Accept the system default. Move cursor to the next line and key in the statement option, if other than 1, the default. Next key in TTC and sequence number. Finally key in SSN preceded by a 0. Press "ENTER." (One of the other options would be selected in order to correct erroneous information contained in the Marine's Master Record. See paragraph (5), below, for a detailed explanation of correction procedures.)

(a) Specific pre-formatted screens are obtained by entering the TTC and sequence numbers. If a specific TTC and sequence number is selected erroneously, key in an exclamation point (!) at the cursor and you will return to the previous screen.

(b) The use of action statements not contained in the TTC-sequence number listing, is not authorized for the OLDS. A STAND ALONE HISTORY STATEMENT can be produced by keying in HIS as the TTC.

(2) 2-GROUP. Key in a 2. Move cursor to the next line and key in the statement option, if other than 1, the default. Next key in TTC and sequence number. Finally key in the two-digit group number. Option 6 can be selected if the group entry is already on the diary and the preparer needs only to add the names of the people to be included in the group entry. (One of the other options would be selected in order to correct erroneous information contained in master records. See paragraph (5), below, for a detailed explanation of correction procedures.)

(3) 3-EVENT. Key in a 3. Move cursor to the next line and key in the statement option if other than 1, the default. Option 1 is accepted in order to input a new event entry. Next key in TTC and sequence number. Finally key in the two-digit event number. (One of the other options would be selected in order to correct erroneous information contained in master record. See paragraph (5), below, for a detailed explanation of correction procedures.)

(4) 4-EXCLUSION. Key in a 4. Move cursor to the next line and key in the statement option if other than 1, the default. Option 1 is accepted in order to input a new exclusion entry. Next key in TTC and sequence number. Then key in the two-digit event number. Finally key in the two-digit exclusion number. Option 6 can be selected if the event entry is already on the diary and the preparer needs only to add the names of the people to be included in the exclusion entry. (One of the other options will be selected in order to correct an error. See paragraph (5) below for a detailed explanation of correction procedures.)

(5) There are four options available for correcting errors.

(a) CORRECTION. This option is used to delete an error on the MECF and to input correct information to the master record. Incorrect information detected prior to posting to the Central Master Record will post instead to the MECF. This option is similar to a DEL ADD in the sense that it deletes erroneous information and adds correct information. The distinction of this option is that the deleted information is contained in the MECF rather than the Central Master Record.

(b) DELETE ADD. This option is selected when there is erroneous information in the Central Master Record and no error on the MECF. In other words, the incorrect information did not fail and create an error on the MECF; it successfully posted to the Central Master Record. This option deletes the erroneous information and replaces it with correct information.

(c) DELETE AS ERRONEOUS. This option is selected when erroneous information has posted to the Central Master Record and there is no correct information to replace it. In other words, the incorrect information did not fail and create an error on the MECF; it successfully posted to the Central Master Record. This option deletes the erroneous information.

(d) CORRECT DELETE AS ERRONEOUS. This option deletes an error from the MECF. No incorrect information is contained in the Central Master Record since the transaction failed to the MECF prior to posting to an individual record or records. This option is similar to a DEL AS ERR in the sense that it deletes erroneous information. The distinction of this option is that the deleted information is contained in the MECF, rather than the Central Master Record.

(e) When using Options 2 and 5 of the above menu to correct errors on the MECF, the preparer will be presented with a screen asking for a Master Error Control Number (MECN) of the error being corrected (JUMPS/MMS only. See chapter 9, RESPRIM, for REMMPS). The seven-digit MECN shown on the error report must be entered. The SSN and MECN entered on this screen must be in agreement with the SSN and MECN on the error report.

(f) In selecting one of these options, the preparer should always consult his applicable manuals (PRIM, RESPRIM,..) to see what kind of correction entry may be required for a particular TTC.

(6) 5-MASTER MENU. Key in a 5 and press "ENTER."

(a) The On-line Diary Clerk Master Function Menu will be displayed on the screen. Select Option 99 and press "ENTER." The On-line Diary Master Menu will be displayed on the screen. Press the "CLEAR" key, the COMPLETE screen will appear. Enter *ULOG OFF and press "ENTER." The Quantico (or local RASC) applications screen will appear., Key in *ULOG OFF, and press "ENTER" to exit the system entirely.

(b) A "LOG-OFF SUCCESSFUL" message should be displayed.

(7) 6-MASTER FUNCTION MENU. Key in a 6 and press "ENTER." Selection of this option will return the system to the Master Function Menu.

e. After selecting options 1 or 2, press "ENTER" and the Diary Update Screen will appear.

```
              REAL FAMMIS ON-LINE DIARY SYSTEM - DIARY UPDATE

          DSSN:              DIARY NUMBER:               DIARY DATE:
 OPTION STATEMENT               (EXCEPTIONS)  SEQ   TIC 698 (POE) SEQUENCE ONLY

  1.... NORMAL                                001 - TO ACCRUE ALL AT CENTRAL.
  2.... DEL AND ADD (CORR) (ACDU ONLY)        002 - TO FOREIGN FINANCIAL.
  3.... DEL AS ERR (DEL)                      003 - FOR DIRECT DEPOSIT.
  4.... CORRECTION (MECF)  (ACDU ONLY)        004 - MAIL TO MILITARY ADDRESS.
  5.... DEL AS ERR (MECF)  (ACDU ONLY)        005 - MAIL TO ANOTHER PERSON/ADDR
  6.... MASTER MENU                           006 - QUARTERS ADDRESS.
  7.... MASTER FUNCTION MENU                  007 - CASH PAYMENT (DECENTRAL).
                                              008 - CHECK PAYMENT (DECENTRAL).
                                              009 - FINAL PAYMENT.

 SELECT STATEMENT OPTION === 1
  INPUT TTC AND SEQUENCE ===          (ENTER 698 AND SEQ FOR POE'S)
  SOCIAL SECURITY NUMBER ===
          EFFECTIVE DATE ===          (USED FOR 698 POE'S ONLY)
-------------------------------------------------------------------
UDD0100A - ENTER THE APPROPRIATE DATA ABOVE FOR YOUR DESIRED OPTIONS.
AFTER ENTERING THE NECESSARY INFORMATION, DEPRESS THE "ENTER" KEY
TO CONTINUE.
```

(1) 1 - NORMAL. Note that the system default is 1. This is the option that is accepted in order to input new information on an individual. (One of the other options would be selected in order to correct erroneous information contained in the Marine's Central Master Record, or to correct an error on the Master Error Control File (MECF). See below for a detailed explanation of correction procedures.)

(a) Input the desired three-digit TTC and three-digit sequence number. Press "ENTER." The next screen to appear will be the input screen for the TTC desired. Each TTC has its own self-prompted input screen. (Note: If a history statement is desired, type in YES, press "ENTER", and the HISTORY INPUT screen will be displayed for the history statement to be entered.)

(b) To input a pay option election (POE) transaction, enter the TTC and sequence number 698 000. Press "ENTER." The POE Menu will appear next.

(2) 2 - DEL AND ADD (CORR). This option is selected when there is erroneous information in the Central Master Record and no error on the MECF. In other words, the incorrect information did not fail and create an error on the MECF; it successfully posted to the master record. This option deletes the erroneous information and replaces it with correct information.

(a) Input the desired three-digit TTC and three-digit sequence number. Press "ENTER." The next screen to appear will be the input screen for the TTC desired.

(b) Each TTC has its own self-prompted input screen. (Note: If a history statement is desired, type in YES, press "ENTER", and the HISTORY INPUT screen will be displayed for the history statement to be entered.)

(3) 3 - DEL AS ERR (DEL). This option is selected when erroneous information has posted to the Central Master Record and there is no correct information to replace it. In other words, the incorrect information did not fail and create an error on the MECF; it successfully posted to the Central Master Record. This option deletes the erroneous information.

(a) Input the desired three-digit TTC and three-digit sequence number. Press "ENTER." The next screen to appear will be the input screen for the TTC desired.

(b) Each TTC has its own self-prompted input screen.

(4) 4 - CORRECTION (MECF). This option is used to delete an error on the MECF and to input correct information to the Central Master Record. No incorrect information is contained in the Central Master Record since the transaction failed to the MECF prior to posting to the individual record. This option is similar to a DEL ADD (CORR) in the sense that it deletes erroneous information and adds correct information. The distinction of this option is that the deleted information is contained in the MECF, rather than the Central Master Record.

(a) Input the desired three-digit TTC and three-digit sequence number. Press "ENTER." The next screen to appear will be the input screen for deleting the error from the MECF and the input screen for the TTC desired to correct the error.

(b) Each TTC has its own self-prompted input screen. (Note: If a history statement is desired, type in YES, press "ENTER", and the HISTORY INPUT screen will be displayed for the history statement to be entered.)

(5) 5 - DEL AS ERR (MECF). This option deletes an error from the MECF. No incorrect information is contained in the Central Master Record since the transaction failed to the MECF prior to posting to an individual record. This option is similar to a DEL AS ERR (DEL) in the sense that it deletes erroneous information. The distinction of this option is that the deleted information is contained in the MECF, rather than the Central Master Record.

(6) 6 - MASTER MENU. Key in a 6 and press "ENTER."

(a) The On-line Diary Master Menu will be displayed. Press the "CLEAR" key. From the COM-PASS screen, key in *ULOG OFF, and press "ENTER."

(b) A "LOG-OFF SUCCESSFUL" message should be displayed.

(c) Press the "ERASE EOF" key or "CLEAR" key. A terminal should not be left until this process has been successfully executed.

(7) 7 - MASTER FUNCTION MENU. Key in a 7 and press "ENTER." Selection of this option will return the system to the Master Function Menu.

2. 20-CHANGE OWN ELECTRONIC SIGNATURE SEED. If you believe your ELSIG has been compromised select this option and the Change ELSIG SEED screen will be displayed (see figure 2-3).

a. Key in current SEED and select a new SEED. Press "ENTER."

b. Memorize your new ELSIG and SEED.

c. Press "ENTER." You will be returned to the Master

Function Menu.

4. 99-TERMINATE ON-LINE SYSTEM. Key in 99 and press "ENTER." The On-line Diary Master Menu will be displayed. Log-off the system using the procedures set forth in chapter 1, subparagraph 1008.1.

Chapter 3

SECTION 3: USER COMMUNICATION METHODS

3301. Message Switching. This is a means of communication between On-line Diary users. In order to send and receive messages, a user must have a User Identification Code. Complete the following procedures to send a message: 1) Sign onto the On-line Diary System using the procedures set forth in chapter 1, paragraph 1005. 2) At the COMPLETE COM-PASS screen, select Option B and press "ENTER." The COMPLETE MESSAGE SWITCHING screen will appear with a choice of 3 options (see figure 3-1). 3) Key in "MS" (without the quotations), press "ENTER." The SEND MESSAGE SWITCHING screen will appear with a choice of 4 options (see figure 3-2). 4) Key in "SI" (without the quotations), press "ENTER." The MESSAGE SWITCHING FUNCTION screen will appear. This is where the user inputs the message to be sent. 5) Key in "SU" (without the quotations) and the User Identification Code of the person who will be receiving your message. 6) Next, type in your message. Once the message you wish to send is completed, press "ENTER." The MESSAGE SWITCHING FUNCTION screen will appear again, but this time it will indicate in the upper right-hand corner that your message has been sent (see figure 3-3). 7) To exit the system, press "CLEAR" until you arrive at the COMPLETE COM-PASS screen. 8) Sign off using the procedures set forth in chapter 1, paragraph 1008. The transmitted message will appear right after the COMPLETE BROADCAST screen appears once the user signs onto the On-line Diary System (see figure 3-4). The message will show the date the message was sent, the message number, and Identification Code of the originator. 9) To acknowledge receipt of the message, press "ENTER" (see figure 3-5).

```
08:29:55     TID 1382       COMPLETE    USER ID GMPI49       01/06/86
                    -- MESSAGE SWITCHING --                     UMY0
          MENU                                              ID    PFK
      -------------------------------------------------------------
      MESSAGE SENDING                                       MS      1
      MESSAGE (RE-) DISPLAY AND HANDLING                    MH      2
      TERMINAL CHARACTERISTICS HANDLING                     TH      3
                          SELECT FUNCTION:                    OR PFK
COM-PASS MESSAGE SWITCHING FACILITY INCLUDES:
- SENDING MESSAGES TO USERS, A GROUP OF USERS, TIDS OR A GROUP OF
  TIDS.
- RETRIEVING, PURGING, DELETING, RE-ROUTING, REPEATING, HOLDING
  AND RELEASING MESSAGES.
- HANDLING I/O STATUS OF TERMINALS, SUCH AS ENABLING, DISABLING
  FOR I/O, SET AN ALTERNATE DESTINATION, ETC.
```

Figure 3-1.--Sample COMPLETE Message Switching Menu Screen.

```
08:29:55     TID 1382       COMPLETE    USER ID GMPI49       01/06/86
                    -- MESSAGE SWITCHING --                     UMY1
          SEND MESSAGE MENU                                 ID    PFK
      -------------------------------------------------------------
      SEND MESSAGE TO USER(S) OR TID(S) OR ALL              SI      1
      SEND MESSAGE TO USERS (SELECT FROM MENU)              SL      2
      SEND MESSAGE TO USER ACCOUNTING GROUP(S)              SG      3
      SEND MESSAGE TO TIDGROUP(S)                           ST      4
                          SELECT FUNCTION:                    OR PFK
MESSAGES ARE SENT TO USER GROUPS, TIDGROUPS OR SELECTED USERS
WITH A SECURITY CLASS CODE.  CLASS CODES SHOULD BE GIVEN AS A
LIST OF CODES SEPARATED BY COMMAS.
- CLASS 1 MESSAGES, STANDARD CLASS, DO NOT INTERRUPT ANY PROGRAM
  (DEFAULT).
- CLASS 2 MESSAGES, URGENT CLASS, PROGRAM WILL BE INTERRUPTED.
- CLASS 3 MESSAGES, SPECIAL PURPOSE CLASS, SAME AS CLASS 2, BUT
  ARE KEPT UNTIL THE NEXT RESTART OF COM-PLETE.
- CLASS 4 MESSAGES, COM-PLETE SYSTEM CLASS, NOT FOR GENERAL USAGE.
MESSAGES THAT ARE SENT TO USERS WHO ARE NOT LOGGED ON WILL BE PUT
IN THEIR MAILBOX, I.E., THEY WILL RECEIVE THE MESSAGE AT THEIR
NEXT LOG-ON.
```

Figure 3-2.--Sample COMPLETE Message Switching Send Message Menu Screen.

```
08:29:55     TID 1382       COMPLETE     USER ID GMPI49      01/06/86
                    -- MESSAGE SWITCHING --                      UM00
    FUNCTION                 ID     PFK         OPERANDS
-------------------------   --     ---    --------------------------
    SEND MESSAGE TO USER     SU       1    MESSAGE (USER ID(S))
                                           (CLASS CODES)
    SEND MESSAGE TO TID      ST       2    MESSAGE (TID NBR(S))
                                           (CLASS CODES)
SEND MESSAGE TO ALL TIDS     SA       3    MESSAGE (CLASS CODES)
   SELECT FUNCTION:             OR PFK
      AND OPERANDS
TO FOLLOWING USERS OR TIDS:  GMPI54
MESSAGE:  THIS IS A TEST.
MESSAGE WILL BE SENT BY CLASS CODES: 1    LAST MSG SEGMENT: Y
UM0000 - MESSAGE (SEGMENT) 21058 HAS BEEN SENT
```

Figure 3-3.--Sample COMPLETE Message Switching Function Screen (With Message).

```
MSG ID: 21058, SENT 01/06/86 AT 832, MY USER GMPI49
THIS IS A TEST.
```

Figure 3-4.--Example of a Message Sent Via COMPLETE Message Switching Menu.

```
ZMS0007 - MSG ID 021058 ACKNOWLEDGED.
```

Figure 3-5.--Example Acknowledgement of a Message Received Via COMPLETE Message Switching Menu.

Chapter 4

CERTIFIER'S INSTRUCTIONS

SECTION 1: OVERVIEW OF FUNCTIONS

4101. Introduction. The certifier is the responsible official assigned by the commanding officer (CO) to review, certify, decertify and sign diaries. The certifier may also print diaries and change his P-ELSIG.

4102. Review and Certify A Diary. In this process the certifier may review and delete entries from an uncertified diary, but cannot add entries. Certifier's must ensure that they review each diary either on-line or hard copy prior to certification. The final diary will be printed, signed and submitted in accordance with current directives after the diary statistics report indicates that it has been closed or processed.

4103. Decertify A Certified Diary. When a diary has been certified and it is discovered that an error exists on the diary any certifier in the unit may decertify the diary. After the required corrective action is accomplished the diary must be recertified. The certifier who recertifies the diary will now be the certifier for all the entries on this diary. This action may not be accomplished after the certified diary has been processed.

4104. Change Own Electronic Signature SEED. The SEED combined with the individual's SSN generates the Certifier's ELSIG. If the certifier believes the ELSIG has been compromised, the SEED should be changed and a new ELSIG generated. For security reasons it is advisable to change your SEED and generate a new ELSIG every sixty (60) days.

Chapter 4

SECTION 2: DETAILED INSTRUCTIONS

4201. Certifier's Entry Process. To enter the certifier's function, use the following steps:

1. Log-on the system using the procedures set forth in chapter 1, paragraph 1005.

2. Key in your ELSIG, SEED, and RUC. Press "ENTER." (NOTE: The ELSIG and SEED will not be displayed due to security reasons.)

4202. Options Available. The following options are available:

10-REVIEW-CERTIFY-DECERTIFY DIARY TRANSACTIONS 20-CHANGE OWN ELECTRONIC SIGNATURE SEED 99-TERMINATE ON-LINE SYSTEM

1. 10-REVIEW-CERTIFY-DECERTIFY DIARY TRANSACTIONS. Upon selection of this option the following screen will be displayed.

```
            REAL FAMMIS ON-LINE DIARY SYSTEM MASTER MENU

*1.  START A NEW DIARY           (PREPARER ONLY)    (DEFAULT=N/A)
*2.  CONTINUE A DIARY            (PREPARER ONLY)    (DEFAULT=NONE)
*3.  REVIEW A DIARY              (PREPARER ONLY)    (DEFAULT=NONE)
        THERE ARE NO DIARIES AVAILABLE FOR REVIEW.
-----------------------------------------------------------------------
 4.  REVIEW AND CERTIFY A DIARY  (CERTIFIER ONLY)   (DEFAULT=00003)
 5.  DECERTIFY A DIARY           (CERTIFIER ONLY)   (DEFAULT=N/A)
-----------------------------------------------------------------------
 6.  PRINT A DIARY            (PRESS PF2 TO SEE AVAILABLE DIARIES)
-----------------------------------------------------------------------
 SELECT DESIRED OPTION ===  4
   INPUT DIARY NUMBER ===        (LEAVE BLANK TO ACCEPT DEFAULT
                                  NUMBER)
    INPUT DIARY DATE ===  840214 (USED FOR OPTION 1 ONLY)

    PRINTER ===  0223    (ENTER TID TO ALTER PRINT DESTINATION)
---PF1 = MASTER FUNCTION MENU PF2 = DIARY STATISTICS REPORT
UDAMENUA - ENTER THE APPROPRIATE DATA ABOVE FOR THE OPTION
DESIRED. ONCE YOU HAVE ENTERED THE DATA NEEDED, DEPRESS THE "ENTER"
KEY TO CONTINUE.
```

*Not applicable to Certifier.

a. 4-REVIEW AND CERTIFY A DIARY. Accept the system default and press "ENTER" if you desire to review/certify the system default diary. If you desire to review/certify another diary listed, position the cursor to the input diary number field and key in the desired diary number. Press "ENTER." The following ELSIG/SEED RE-ENTRY screen will appear prior to actual certification/deletion of a diary:

```
        REAL FAMMIS ON-LINE DIARY SYSTEM ELSIG/SEED RE-ENTRY
                      CERTIFICATION/DELETION
DSSN:                  DIARY NUMBER:          DIARY DATE:

1.  THIS DIARY WAS LAST TOUCHED AT 09:30:06 ON 14 FEB 84.  IF YOU
    WANT TO REVIEW THIS DIARY PRIOR TO TAKING ANY ACTION, PLEASE
    ENTER (YES) WITHOUT ENTERING YOUR ELSIG AND SEED.

2.  IF YOU WANT TO CERTIFY/DELETE THIS DIARY, PLEASE RE-ENTER YOUR
    ELSIG AND SEED.

3.  ONCE YOU HAVE ENTERED YOUR ELSIG AND SEED, DEPRESS THE "ENTER"
    KEY.

4.  IF YOU DO NOT WANT TO PERFORM THIS FUNCTION AT THIS TIME,
    LEAVE YOUR ELSIG AND SEED BLANK THEN DEPRESS YOUR "ENTER" KEY.

    DO YOU WANT TO REVIEW?  NO

           ELSIG:

           SEED:
```

If the DATE-TIME-GROUP on the above screen matches the DATE-TIME-GROUP of the reviewed hard copy diary, certifier may take the NO option without reviewing each page of the diary. If the certifier desires to review each page of a diary, follow the instructions of Option 1 on the screen.

(1) If Option 1 is selected, the diary will be displayed with the statements listed as they were entered. Use the "TAB FIELD FORWARD" key to advance to each statement.

(a) To delete a statement, key in a "D", press "ENTER", and the statement will be deleted.

(b) If no statements are marked for deletion or review, press "ENTER" to advance to the next page of the diary. A system default will always cause the next page of the diary to be displayed. After the entire diary has been reviewed the Certification screen will be displayed. If you desire to exit the review process prior to reviewing each page of the diary move the cursor to the field following CONTINUE and key in NO. Press "ENTER." You will be returned to the Master Function Menu.

(c) After the review process has been completed you can certify the diary by entering your ELSIG and SEED on the Certification screen. If you do not desire to certify the diary, leave the screen blank and press "ENTER." You will be returned to the Master Function Menu.

(d) A diary can be deleted in its entirety by deleting all of the transactions on the diary and then entering the certification process. If the diary is empty; that is, if all of the entries have been deleted, then the certification process will cause a deletion screen to appear. A certifier can enter his ELSIG and SEED on the screen and delete the entire diary. If you do not wish to delete the diary leave the ELSIG and SEED blank and press "ENTER." You will be returned to the Master Function Menu. An entire diary should be deleted only in the case where an incorrect diary number or date is selected to start a new diary. For example, if diary 983 were started and the desired diary number was actually 9, then diary 983 could be deleted in its entirety.

b. 5-DECERTIFY A DIARY. Key in 5 and press "ENTER" if you desire to decertify the system default diary. If you desire to decertify another diary listed, position the cursor to the input diary number field and key in the desired diary number, press "ENTER." The ELSIG SEED RE-ENTRY decertification screen will be displayed. Key in your ELSIG and SEED and press "ENTER." If you do not desire to decertify the diary, leave the ELSIG and SEED blank and press "ENTER." You will be returned to the Master Function Menu.

c. 6-PRINT A DIARY. Key in 6 in the option field and the desired diary number in the INPUT DIARY NUMBER field. (Upon selection of option PF2, all diaries available for print, and their status will be displayed and are available for print for fifteen (15) days after the cycle date reflected on the Diary Statistics Report. Extreme care must be taken to ensure that diaries are printed prior to the drop-off date. Failure to do so will result in the unit being unable to print diaries. Commanders should contact the ACU for assistance when they are unable to print diaries. To return to the Master Function Menu, press "ENTER.")

2. <u>20-CHANGE OWN ELECTRONIC SIGNATURE SEED</u>. If you believe your ELSIG has been compromised, this option should be selected.

a. Key in current SEED and select and new SEED. Press "ENTER." A new ELSIG will be generated.

b. Memorize the new ELSIG and SEED. Press "ENTER." The Master Function Menu will be displayed.

3. <u>99 - TERMINATE ON-LINE SYSTEM</u>. Key in 99 and press "ENTER." The On-line Diary Master Menu will be displayed. Log-off the system using the procedures set forth in chapter 1, subparagraph 1008.1.

Chapter 5

REPORTS AND PROCEDURES

SECTION 1: PROCEDURES FOR PRINTING REPORTS

5101. General. The standardized feedback reports, outlined in section 1 of this chapter, can be printed by selecting an option for each report on the On-line Diary Master Menu.

5102. Sign-On/Log-On. To access the On-line Diary Master Menu, follow the procedures set forth in chapter 1, paragraph 1006.

5103. On-line Diary Master Menu. The following options are available on the On-line Diary Master Menu. To review a report, the user will key in the desired option, the applicable parameters and press "ENTER." For printing error reports, enter "C", followed by the RUC, move the cursor down to SCYCNR and press the "ERASE EOF" key to remove the zeroes. To print advisory reports, enter "D" followed by the RUC, then enter the cycle number.

Option	Description	Parameters
A	Diary System	
B	Diary Statistics Report	RUC/DSSN
C	Error Report	RUC/DSSN
D	Advisory Report	RUC/DSSN, (SCYCNR)
E	Unit/Disbursing Reports	RUC/DSSN
F	MPV/MPL Statistics Report	DSSN
G	TTC/SEQ REPORT (BY TTC/SEQ)	
H	TTC/SEQ REPORT (BY ENGLISH)	

```
     OPTION:
        RUC:
       DSSN:
 PAYROLL NR:
     SCYCNR: 000  LAST COMPLETED:  009 860119
     PRTOPT: (USED WITH OPTION C/D ONLY)
    PRTDEST:
```

5104. Print Reports. There are two methods of printing reports. 1) The user must first enter the desired option, the RUC or DSSN, and press "ENTER." The first page of the selected report will appear on the screen for review. To print the first page of the report, the user must turn the printer on, and press the local print key. On most terminals the local print key is either the "PA2" key or a special key marked with a special symbol. This key causes the current screen to be printed. By depressing the local print key the first page of the report will be printed. To print subsequent pages of the report, press "ENTER", wait for the new page to appear on the screen, and then press the local print key. 2) The second method is to select the desired Option, the RUC or DSSN. Move the cursor down to "PRTOPT" and enter "Y." Enter the printer destination code at "PRT DEST", and press "ENTER." The requested report will print out in it's entirety at the requested printer location.

5105. Sign-off Procedures. To exit the On-line Diary Master Menu, log-off the system using the procedures set forth in chapter 1, subparagraph 1008.2.

Chapter 5

SECTION 2: PROCEDURES FOR PRINTING PERSONNEL/DISBURSING REPORTS

5201. General. The standardized feedback personnel and disbursing reports outlined in Section 1 of this chapter can be printed by selecting an option for each report on the Unit/Disbursing Reports Menu.

5202. Sign-On/Log-On. To access the Unit/Disbursing Reports Menu, use the same sign-on procedures for accessing the On-line Diary Master Menu. When the Diary Master Function Menu appears on the screen, select Option "E" for Unit/Disbursing Reports and PRESS "ENTER." The following menu will appear on the screen:

UNIT/DISBURSING REPORTS

OPTION	PARAMETERS	DESCRIPTION
A	RUC	Unit Verification Roster
B	RUC	Unit Alpha Personnel Roster
C	RUC	Unit Personnel Roster by SSN
D	RUC	Unit Personnel Roster by Rank
E	RUC, LSSN	Unit Annual Audit Roster
F	DSSN, BCYC (ECYC)	System Exception Report
G	RUC	Record of Emergency Data

OPTION:	
RUC:	
DSSN:	
LSSN:	(LAST DIGIT OF SSN)
BCYC:	
ECYC:	(MAXIMUM RANGE OF 5 CYCLES,
RECEIVING RUC:	IE.; 001-005)
ADDITIONAL ROUTING INFO:	(DEST OF REPORT BEING PRINTED)

5203. Unit/Disbursing Reports Menu. To request a report on the Unit/Disbursing Reports Menu, the user will key in the desired option, the required parameters and press "ENTER." If the parameters are correctly entered, the following advisory message will appear on the screen: "Your job has been successfully submitted. Your printed report will be distributed by the RASC/ACU."

5204. Procedures for Printing/Distributing Reports. The unit will request reports on the Unit/Disbursing Reports Menu. The requested report will process in a batch mode at central, and will be electronically transmitted to a high-speed printer at the Regional Automated Service Center (RASC) in the local jurisdiction for printing and distribution. The ACU will obtain personnel reports from the RASC and distribute them to the unit. Inquiries concerning the printing and distribution of personnel reports will be directed to the ACU.

5205. Return to Master Menu. To return to the OLDS Master Menu, press the "CLEAR" key.

5206. Sign-Off Procedures. To exit the Unit/Disbursing Reports Menu, log-off the System using the procedures set forth in chapter 1, subparagraph 1008.2.

Chapter 6

USER'S RESEARCH OPTIONS

SECTION 1: DIARY RETRIEVAL SYSTEM (DRS)

6101. Purpose. The Diary Retrieval System enables the user to review all diary and TODE transactions that have been processed at the Marine Corps Central Design and Programming Activity (MCCDPA), Kansas City, MO. It also contains all of the errors and advisory messages created during the processing of these transactions.

6102. Composition. The Diary Retrieval System is composed of the following data files:

1. Transaction Researcher File.

2. Master Error Control File.

3. Advisory File.

6103. Retrieval System Access. Sign onto the system following the instructions contained in chapter 1, paragraph 1006. From the KCMOPROD COMPASS screen, key in Option A (VIS), and press the "PF7" key. The Diary Retrieval System Menu will be displayed. Certain type retrieval keys may be selected and entered in the type retrieval key field to view the following:

1. Transaction Researcher File. Key 01 through 08 and the appropriate parameters to retrieve diary/TODE records from the Transaction Researcher File (TRF). Transactions will appear on the TRF for approximately four months.

2. Master Error Control File. Key 10 through 16 and the appropriate parameters to retrieve error records from the Master Error Control File (MECF).

3. Advisory File. Key 20 through 27 and the appropriate parameters to retrieve advisory message records from the Advisory File (ADF).

4. Combined File. Key 30 and the appropriate parameters to retrieve record displays combining all three files (TRF, MECF, ADF) into one display screen per TTC entry.

5. Users Instructions Guidelines. Key 60 to retrieve additional information about the Diary Retrieval System (DRS).

6104. Data Entry. Certain parameter fields must be completed, depending on the option selected. For example, Option 01 requires entry of the RUC, DNR, SSN and TTC, while Option 03 requires only the RUC and DNR. Parameters in brackets are optional. If any field is omitted or erroneously entered, an asterisk will be displayed next to the element in addition to a message advising that the required field must be entered/corrected. Upon completion of the required fields, press "ENTER." When changing the option, it is not necessary to delete the existing parameter fields displayed from the previous retrieval. Those fields not required will not be "read" when a request is processed, even though they may contain data from a previous request.

6105. Return to On-line Diary Master Menu. Press the "CLEAR" key and the KCMOPROD COM-PASS screen will appear. Enter *ULOG OFF, and press "ENTER."

Chapter 6

SECTION 2: VIDEO INQUIRY SYSTEM (VIS)

6201. Purpose. The VIS provides users with procedures to access and review JUMPS/MMS/REMMPS data on individual Marines. Instructions as to the operation and different menus available are contained in the current edition of MCO P5200.22, Marine Corps Video Inquiry System User's Manual, (MCVISUM).

6202. Retrieval System Access. Sign onto the system following the instructions contained in chapter 1, paragraph 1006. From the KCMOPROD COM-PASS screen, enter Option A (VIS), and press "ENTER" (see figure 6-1). To gain access to the JUMPS/MMS/REMMPS VIS, press the "ALT" key and the "PF3" key simultaneously for JUMPS/MMS or "PF4" key for REMMPS. Once in the VIS, the user may elect any of the menus offered on the screen (see figure 6-2 or figure 6-3).

6203. Return to the KCMOPROD COM-PASS Menu. Press the "CLEAR" key, and the KCMOPROD COM-PASS screen will appear. Enter *ULOG OFF, and press "ENTER." The terminal is now completely logged off the system.

```
*VIS  THE VIDEO INQUIRY SYSTEM (VIS) WAS DEVELOPED TO GIVE
FUNCTIONAL AND TECHNICAL USERS RANDOM ON-LINE RECORD RETRIEVAL
FROM MASTER FILES MAINTAINED AT THE MCCDPA, KANSAS CITY.  ACCESS
TO THESE FILES AND THE SPECIFIC DATA NEEDED IS ACHIEVED BY
APPROPRIATE USER RESPONSE TO THE MENU SCREENS PROVIDED.  THE MENU
SCREENS GIVE A BRIEF DESCRIPTION OF THE DISPLAYS AVAILABLE FOR
EACH FILE AND THE COMMANDS NEEDED TO RETRIEVE A DISPLAY.  FOR
COMPREHENSIVE INSTRUCTIONS ON USE OF THE VIDEO INQUIRY SYSTEM AND
DETAILED DESCRIPTIONS OF THE COMMANDS NECESSARY FOR A DISPLAY
REQUEST, CONSULT THE CDPA VIS USER'S MANUAL.

     IF YOU WANT:                   DEPRESS:       OR ENTER:
     THE BONDS/ALLOTMENTS MENU       PF1            *BAMENU
     THE RETIRED PAY MENU            PF2            *RPMENU
     THE JUMPS/MMS MENU              PF3            *JPMENU
     THE REMMPS MENU                 PF4            *RMMENU
     THE COMMON MENU                 PF5            *COMENU
     THE AUTODIN MENU                PF6            *ADMENU
     THE DRS MENU                    PF7            *DRMENU
```

Figure 6-1.--Sample Video Inquiry System Menu Screen.

```
JPMENU  THE FIVE MOST COMMONLY USED DISPLAYS FOR     01/06/86
        JUMPS/MMS FILE ARE DESCRIBED BELOW.  THERE   07:14:31
        ARE SEVERAL SPECIALIZED DISPLAYS ALSO AVAILABLE
        WHICH ARE CONTAINED IN "DOCU."
JP## - REPLACE ## WITH A VALUE 01 THRU 12 DEPENDING ON THAT
       PART OF THE JUMPS/MMS RECORD DESIRED.
J### - DISPLAYS THE JUMPS REMARKS RECORDS.  REPLACE ### WITH
       THE REMARK NUMBER DESIRED.
JRZ# - DISPLAYS THE JUMPS CONTROL RECORD ZERO.  REPLACE #
       WITH A VALUE 0 THRU 5.
JQSN - DISPLAYS THE QUOTA MASTER FILE.  ENTER THE QUOTA
       SERIAL NUMBER IN THE SSN FIELD.
DOCU - DISPLAYS THE ON-LINE DOCUMENTATION FOR THE JUMPS/MMS.

 ENTER THE REQUESTED DISPLAY:
               ENTER THE SSN:

 PF1 - B&A     PF3 - JUMPS/MMS    PF5 - COMMON    PF7 - DRS
 PF2 - RETPAY  PF4 - REMMPS       PF6 - AUTODIN
```

Figure 6-2.--Sample JUMPS/MMS VIS Menu Screen.

```
*RMMENU     A BRIEF DESCRIPTION OF DISPLAYS AVAILABLE        03/13/86
            FOR THE REMMPS MASTER FILE ARE LISTED BELOW      09:21:22
 MIND - DISPLAYS SUMMARY OF REMMPS INFORMATION AVAILABLE FOR
        REQUESTED SSN.
 MSXY - DISPLAYS THE REMMPS INFORMATION FOR PAGE Y WITHIN
        SEGMENT X.
 SRRR - DISPLAYS A SUMMARY LISTING FOR REMMPS REMARK - RRR.
 MRRR - REQUIRES OCCURRENCE NR BE ENTERED, WILL DISPLAY THE
        REMARK REQUESTED.
 MSQC - REMMPS SEGMENT QUALITY CONTROL.
 RRED - DISPLAYS THE REMMPS RECORD OF EMERGENCY DATA.

 ENTER THE REQUESTED DISPLAY:  MSQC
               ENTER THE SSN:
OCCURRENCE NR (IF NECESSARY):  001
            AUTOMATIC PAGING:  NO

   PF1 - B&A     PF3 - JUMPS/MMS     PF5 - COMMON     PF7 - DRS
   PF2 - RETPAY  PF4 - REMMPS        PF6 - AUTODIN    PF8 - OLD
```

Figure 6-3.--Sample REMMPS VIS Menu Screen.

APPENDIX A

GLOSSARY OF TERMS

1. COMMANDING OFFICER (CO) ELSIG. A two-part code consisting of a seven-digit alphanumeric sequence generated by the system, plus a three-digit alphanumeric sequence (SEED) determined by the CO. This code is created by the CO using the MASTER ELSIG which has been pre-assigned to his unit to certify/decertify diaries. The CO ELSIG is considered a personal signature and should be maintained as such.

2. CERTIFIER'S ELSIG. A personal ELSIG, which is assigned by the CO. This ELSIG allows the individual to access the certifying officer's functions and to certify/decertify diaries.

3. CURSOR. A symbol which indicates a particular position on the screen. A letter or symbol keyed in by the operator will be placed in the position indicated by the cursor.

4. DEFAULT. When a variety of options are available, the OLDS automatically suggests the most commonly used option. The operator should accept the default or key in the desired option prior to pressing "ENTER." This function is provided to allow the operator to progress rapidly through commonly used options.

5. ELSIG (Electronic Signature). A two-part code consisting of a seven-digit alphanumeric sequence generated by the system, plus a three-digit alphanumeric sequence (SEED) determined by the individual. It is used to access the system, identify specific operators, and limit those functions which an operator is authorized to perform. (See Master ELSIG, CO ELSIG, P-ELSIG, Certifier's and Preparer's ELSIG.)

6. ERROR STATEMENT. A message which appears on the upper-left portion of the screen. This message describes an error when the system detects that erroneous information has been input.

Examples:
1. INPUT MUST BE NUMERIC.
2. THIS IS NOT A VALID SSN, REKEY.
3. DIARY HAS INCOMPLETE GROUP OR EXCLUSIVE ENTRIES.

7. FIELD. A logical combination of alphanumeric characters input by the operator, or by default, which combine to form a word, a number or a code. (Examples: SSN, date, TTC and sequence number, last name, etc.)

8. INPUT. Information which is entered into the OLDS via the keyboard.

9. KEYBOARD. The piece of equipment which contains the letters, numbers and symbols by which input is accomplished. The following keys are significant to the OLDS.

ENTER - Used to input the information which the operator has keyed in (placed on the screen) and send it to the computer. Until the ENTER key is pressed, the information is not sent to the computer.

RESET - This key allows the operator to reestablish an input mode in the event the screen "locks" up (i.e., the cursor disappears and the system will not allow input or respond once ENTER has been pressed). This condition should not be confused with a slow response time. (See #18, below.)

ERASE END OF FILE - Erases all the information on the screen which appears to the right and below the cursor.

TAB/FIELD FORWARD KEY - Either of these keys moves the cursor form the field where it is displayed to the beginning of the next field.

10. MASTER ELSIG (M-ELSIG). The electronic signature pre-assigned to a reporting unit. This ELSIG is used by the commanding officer to establish the CO ELSIG. The M-ELSIG is issued by the REAL FAMMIS Electronic Signature Security Officer and maintained by the CO.

11. MENU. A screen display which contains a listing of options available to the operator.

12. OPTION. A specific task which may be selected by an operator from a menu.

13. ON-LINE. Direct electronic input of information displayed on the screen to the central computer located in Kansas City.

14. OUTPUT. Electronic or paper diary produced by the OLDS. There are three stages of output during the diary process. The ROUGH-NOT CERTIFIED DIARY is a diary which has not been certified; the ROUGH-NOT PROCESSED DIARY is a diary which has been certified but not called into the system for processing; and the CLOSED DIARY is a completed diary which has been collected by the CDPA at Kansas City. It may or may not have been processed.

15. PERSONAL ELSIG (P-ELSIG). An ELSIG which is assigned to an individual by the commanding officer. A P-ELSIG is either a CO ELSIG, a Certifier's ELSIG, or a Preparer's ELSIG.

16. PREPARER'S ELSIG. An ELSIG which is assigned by the CO which allows the individual to access the Preparer's functions.

17. PRINTER. The device provided with the OLDS from which paper diaries may be produced. In order to cause a diary to be printed the pre-assigned printer number should be used. This four-digit number, which uniquely identifies a printer, is called the printer designation code.

18. RESET KEY. Pressing this key tells the computer to disregard whatever instruction it is currently working on. Do not use this key if the computer is working on your diary and the response time is slow. Units could lose diaries by using the RESET key in this manner.

19. RESPONSE TIME. The elapsed time between pressing the "ENTER" key and the system responding to the input.

20. SCREEN. The composite "picture" which is displayed on the terminal.

21. SEED. A three-digit alphanumeric sequence which is determined by the operator and is the second increment of an ELSIG. Operators can change their ELSIGS by changing their SEEDS.

22. SEQUENCE NUMBER. The three-digit number which distinguishes the variations of a Type Transaction Code (TTC). The TTC along with the sequence number allows a particular pre-formatted screen to be displayed on the terminal.

23. TTC (Type Transaction Code). A three-digit number which is assigned to each type of transaction utilized within the OLDS. This number, along with a corresponding sequence number, allows the operator to specify the type of diary entry to be input.

Distribution: DX3

Copy to:

CMC (Asst to DC/S for Mpr), Washington, DC 20380-0001	1
CMC (M-1), Washington, DC 20380-0001	1
CMC (MH), Washington, DC 20380-0001	1
CMC (MR), Washington, DC 20380-0001	1
CMC (MMPR), Washington, DC 20380-0001	1
CMC (MMOS), Washington, DC 20380-0001	1
CMC (MMRB), Washington, DC 20380-0001	1
CMC (MMPE), Washington, DC 20380-0001	1
CMC (MMPR), Washington, DC 20380-0001	1
CMC (MMOS), Washington, DC 20380-0001	1
CMC (MMOA), Washington, DC 20380-0001	1
CMC (MMEA), Washington, DC 20380-0001	1
CMC (MPI-10), Washington, DC 20380-0001	1
CMC (MPI-20), Washington, DC 20380-0001	1
CMC (MPI-30), Washington, DC 20380-0001	1
CMC (MPI-40), Washington, DC 20380-0001	5
CMC (MPI-50), Washington, DC 20380-0001	1
CMC (MPI-60), Washington, DC 20380-0001	1
CMC (RESM), Washington, DC 20380-0001	1
CMC (CCI), Washington, DC 20380-0001	1
Dir, MCCDPA (Code 09A), Quantico, VA 22143-5001	1
Dir, MCCDPA (Code 09B), Quantico, VA 22143-5001	1
Dir, MCCDPA (Code 09F), Quantico, VA 22143-5001	1
Dir, MCCDPA (Code TPPS), Kansas City, MO 64197-0501	1
Each ACU	5
CO, MCFC (MPI-LNU), Kansas City, MO 64197-0001	1
CO, MCFC (RFAM), Kansas City, MO 64197-0001	1
CO, MCFC (M), Kansas City, MO 64197-0001	1
CO, NPRDC (Code 61), San Diego, CA 92152-6800	1
CO, NPRDC (Code 622), San Diego, CA 92152-6800	1
Supt, NPS (Code 54Dk), Monterey, CA 93943-5100	1
Supt, NPS (Code 0306), Monterey, CA 93943-5100	1
DSA, 350 Fortune Terrace, Rockville, MD 20854-2995	1
Ideamatics, 1806 T St., N.W., Washington, DC 20009	1
PAC, Suite 350, 1300 N. 17th St., Arlington, VA 22209	1
MTT, Camp Lejeune, NC 28542-0001	1
CO, PA School, Camp Lejeune, NC 28542-0001	1

www.ingramcontent.com/pod-product-compliance
Lightning Source LLC
Chambersburg PA
CBHW081144290526
45795CB00006B/2370

* 9 7 8 1 4 9 1 0 6 6 8 7 4 *